My birthday

A letter

1 Read. Then colour, trace and write.

Hello Tom,

It's my birthday today. I'm seven.
How old are you? My birthday cake is
brown with seven purple candles. My
favourite colour is purple! What's your
favourite colour?

From
Emma

T0344324

1 I'm _____
2 My favourite colour is _____

2 Read and circle.

1 How old is Emma?   *seven* / *eight*
2 What is Emma's favourite colour?   *brown* / *purple*
3 Is the cake orange?   *yes* / *no*
4 What colour are Emma's candles?   *purple* / *pink*

1 Numbers and colours

Read. Then colour.

1 My favourite colour is red.

2 My favourite colour is green.

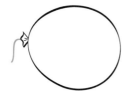

3 My favourite colour is yellow.

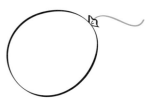

4 My favourite colour is blue.

Match the numbers.

a He is three.

b She is four.

c I am ten.

d Emma is seven.

4

3

7

10

Read. Then trace and colour.

1 Look at Tom's _butterfly_.  It's red and orange.

2 Look at his _bird_. His bird is brown.

3 Look at my _flower_. It's pink and white.

4 Look at Emma's _fish_. Her fish is yellow and black.

Remember!

Names **start with a** capital letter.

Sentences **start with a** capital letter.

His name is **T**om. **H**e's eight.

6 **Read and circle.**

1 (*my* / My) favourite colour is red.

2 (*The* / *the*) butterfly is yellow.

3 (*it's* / *It's*) my birthday today.

4 Tom is eight and (*emma* / *Emma*) is seven.

7 **Write. Use words from the box.**

| eight | fish | Emma | red and black | From | birthday |

Hello ¹ Emma ,

Today is my ² _____ .

I'm ³ _____ .

My favourite present is
a ⁴ _____ .

It's ⁵ _____ .

⁶ _____ Tom

2 At school

Describing a room

1 Read. Then trace and draw.

What's this?
It's a _ruler_ .

1

What's this?
It's a _book_ .

2

What's this?
It's a _pencil_ .

3

What's this?
It's a _desk_ .

4

What's this?
It's a _rubber_ .

5

What's this?
It's a _pen_ .

6

What's this?
It's a _chair_ .

7

8
What's this?

It's a _pencil case_ .

Numbers and classroom objects

② **Read. Then draw.**

1 a pencil sharpener and a rubber   **2** a pen, a pencil case and a pencil

③ **Read. Then write.**

| fifteen | seventeen | eleven | nineteen | fourteen |

¹ *eleven* , twelve, thirteen, ² _____, ³ _____
sixteen, ⁴ _____, eighteen, ⁵ _____, twenty

④ **Read and write. Then draw.**

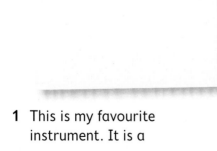

1 This is my favourite
instrument. It is a
_____ .

2 These are in the
music room. They are
_____ .

2 Describing a room

5 Find and count. Then trace.

rubbers [4]

pencils [ ]

rulers [ ]

books [ ]

6 Read and write. Use *they're* and *it's*.

1 They are tables.

They're tables.

2 It is a drum.

_____

3 They are my favourite instruments.

_____

4 It is red and white. What is it?

_____

5 They are red.

_____

6 It is a yellow book.

_____

My family

A picture of my family

1 **Read. Then trace and number.**

1 Hello, I'm Matthew.
I'm seven.
This is my _family_ !

2 This is my _brother_ .
He's eleven.

3 This is my _sister_ .
She's eight.

4 This is my _mum_ .

5 And this is my _dad_ .

2 **Draw your family. Then write.**

Hello, I'm _____ .
I'm _____ . This is my family!

3 Jobs

3 Unscramble. Then write the family members.

1 mmu   *mum*

2 oetrrhb _____

3 add _____

4 eissrt _____

5 nyagnr _____

6 ddnrgaa _____

4 Look. Find six jobs.

B	A	U	A	P	C	V	Z
X	R	D	V	E	T	E	O
A	T	I	G	C	K	D	H
R	I	C	O	O	K	O	Y
W	S	C	O	C	G	C	F
R	T	P	I	L	O	T	D
H	D	Q	E	M	J	O	N
B	F	A	R	M	E	R	K

Remember!

We use a **?** after a question.

Is your mum a vet**?**

5 **Read and write.**

1 Is she a vet?

No, she isn't.

She's a farmer.

2 Is she a teacher?

_____

_____

3 Is she an artist?

_____

_____

4 Is he a cook?

_____

_____

5 Is he a doctor?

_____

_____

6 Is he a farmer?

_____

_____

6 **Circle and write. Then draw.**

My (*mum / dad*) is

_____ .

4 My body

Describing someone

1 Read. Then draw and colour.

Hi, I'm Jenny. This is my brother.

His name is Ben. He's eight.

He's got brown eyes and blond hair.

Look at his favourite clothes!

He's got a red and blue T-shirt.

He's got green shorts and he's got brown and white shoes.

2 Read. Then circle *Yes* or *No*.

1	This is Ben.	Yes / No
2	Ben's got blue eyes.	Yes / No
3	Ben is nine.	Yes / No
4	Ben's got brown and white shorts.	Yes / No
5	Ben's got a red and blue T-shirt.	Yes / No

3 Read. Then draw and colour.

Hi, my name is Ann. I'm seven years old.

I've got blue eyes and brown hair.

I've got my backpack. It's green.

These are my favourite shoes. They're orange.

My skirt is purple and my jumper is red.

4 **Unscramble. Then write and match.**

1 ckoss   *s o c k s*

2 rstthi   _ _ _ _ _ _

3 sseoh   _ _ _ _ _

4 eotssrru   _ _ _ _ _ _ _ _

5 tha   _ _ _

6 riskt   _ _ _ _ _

7 jmrupe   _ _ _ _ _ _

5 **Read and write. Then draw your body.**

1 I've got one body and two a *rms* _____.

2 I've got two l_____.

3 I've got five f_____ on my hand.

4 I've got ten t_____ on my feet.

4 Describing someone

6 Draw. Then write.

This is me.

My name's _____ .

I'm _____ .

I've got _____ eyes and _____ hair.

Look at my favourite clothes.

I've got _____ . I've got _____

_____ and I've got _____ .

① Look. Then read and match.

My book of pets

Contents

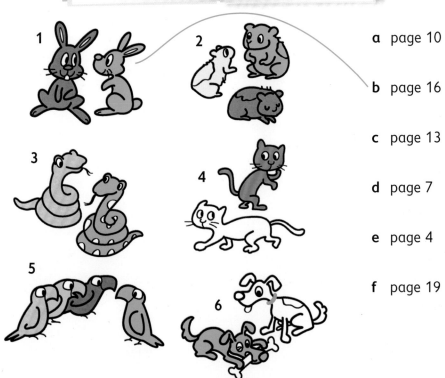

1

2

3

4

5

6

a page 10

b page 16

c page 13

d page 7

e page 4

f page 19

5 Animals / adjectives

② Read and match.

a

1 It's got four legs and a tail.

b

2 It's got two legs and two wings.

c

3 It's got two big ears and a small white tail.

d

4 It's long. It's got no legs.

③ Read. Then draw.

1 a small spider

2 a big spider

3 a short snake

4 a long snake

Remember!

Alphabetical order = **c**at, **d**og, **s**pider

4 **Match. Then write in alphabetical order.**

1	h	ogs	_____
2	s	ats	*cats*
3	r	amsters	_____
4	d	arrots	_____
5	p	abbits	_____
6	c	nakes	_____

5 **Make a pet book. Write the contents.**

My book of pets
_____

Animal	Page
_____	page 1
Parrots	page 3
_____	page ___
_____	page ___
_____	page ___

6 My house

Describing a house

① Read. Then draw.

1

This is my house. It's got four small windows and a big door.

It's got a garden and three trees. There's a mouse in the garden. It's under the tree.

2

This is my house. It's got two small windows and a small door.

It's got flowers in the garden. It's a small garden. It's my favourite garden!

I've got two dogs. Look! They are in the garden.

This is my flat. It's got three windows. It hasn't got a garden.

It's got flowers under the window. There are two flowers. And look! There's a bird on a flower!

3

2 Read. Then write and match.

a

1 This is my cat! He's in the _____.

b

2 There is a shower in the _____.

c

3 There's a fridge in the _____.

d

4 There's a TV in the _____.

3 Find and circle. Then match.

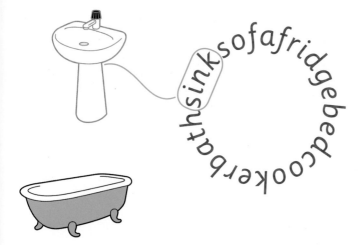

6 Labelling a house

Remember!

Some words have the same sound but different spellings.
house and flower

4 Write (✔) or (✗). Then correct.

1 flowr   ✗   *flower*

2 window   ☐

3 howse   ☐

4 gardin   ☐

5 living room   ☐

6 door   ☐

5 Draw your favourite house. Then label. Use the words from the box.

living room   kitchen   bedroom   bathroom   window   door
bed   sink   cooker   garden   TV   sofa   lamp   bath

Food

A questionnaire

1 **Read. Then write (✔) or (✘) for Rita.**

What food do you like, Rita?
Do you like salad?

No, I don't.

Do you like chicken?

No, I don't.

Do you like fruit?

No, I don't.

What food do you like?

I like cake, chocolate,
ice cream and sweets ...

Wow! What a diet!!!!!

 Questionnaire

Do you like salad?	☐	Do you like fruit?	☐
Do you like chicken?	☐	Do you like ice cream?	☐

2 Read. Then circle the odd one out.

1 (cheese)   water   milk   lemonade

2 cheese   milk   yoghurt   meat

3 sausages   meat   bread   pen

4 lemonade   jelly   water   juice

Read and draw. Then write.

Sue's packed lunch
  chocolate
  sausages
  cake
  lemonade

Tom's packed lunch
  salad
  cheese
  yoghurt
  milk

Emma's packed lunch
  fruit
  chicken
  carrots
  water

My packed lunch

Remember!

Questions start with a capital letter and end with a ?

Do you like sausages?

4 **Read and write (✔) or (✗). Then correct.**

1 Do you like sausages. ☒ *Do you like sausages?*

2 Do you like yoghurt? ☐ _____

3 I like chips? ☐ _____

4 Yes, I do. ☐ _____

5 No, I don't? ☐ _____

6 I don't like carrots. ☐ _____

5 **Write. Then draw.**

Questionnaire

Do you like _milk_ ?

Do you like _____ ?

Do you _____ ?

_____

_____

8 I'm excited

Headlines

1 Read the headlines. Then match.

Tom, Kate, Emma and Ben are in the park.

1 TOM'S EXCITED   **2 EMMA'S BORED**

3 BEN'S ANGRY   **4 KATE'S HAPPY**

a 4

Kate has got Ben's toy car.
Kate wants a toy car for her birthday.
'This is my favourite toy. I like cars.'

b

Kate has got Ben's toy car.
Ben wants it. 'It's my car, Kate!'

c

Emma hasn't got a car
but she's got a ball.

d

It's Tom's birthday. He's in the park.
He's got a bike.
'Look at my new bike!'

2 Read and match.

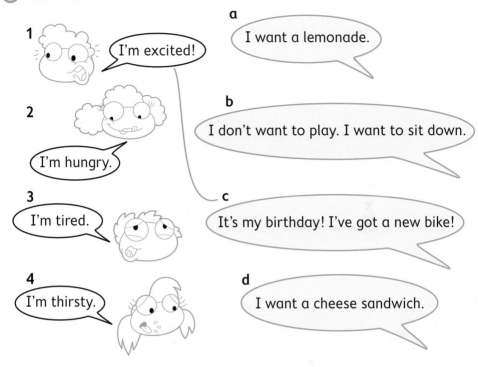

a I want a lemonade.

1 I'm excited!

b I don't want to play. I want to sit down.

2 I'm hungry.

3 I'm tired.

c It's my birthday! I've got a new bike!

4 I'm thirsty.

d I want a cheese sandwich.

3 Look and sort. Then write.

jumper   T-shirt   socks   trousers   hat   dress   scarf   skirt

hot   cold

8 Headlines

4 Read. Then write a headline.

excited   bored   hungry

It's carnival time!
I've got a mask.
It's a rabbit mask.
It's pink and white.

1 ___I'm excited._____

I've got a new kitchen.
I like vegetables and fish.
I like chocolate and fruit!
I like food!

2 _____

My friends are in the garden.
I'm in bed. I'm ill.
I want to play.

3 _____